Messiah vs. False Messiah

Israel's Covenant With Death

ERIKA GREY

Pedante Press

Short Book Series

Messiah vs. False Messiah: Israel's Covenant of Death

DEDICATION

To those who have the eyes to see and the
ears to hear..

CONTENTS

Acknowledgments   i

1   The Covenant   1

2   Covenant with Death   8

3   The Unholy Covenant   13

4   Teachings on the Jewish Messiah   22

5   Mashiach Builds The Third Temple   32

6   Return Jews To Israel and Recognize Torah   43

7   Current Affairs & The Future Treaty   49

8   The False Messiah's Treaty   59

9   The Abomination of Desolation   64

10   The 1260-1290 Days of Daniel   71

www.erikagrey.com

For Bible Prophecy news and analysis and
more books visit my website.

1 THE COVENANT

The False Messiah signs a comprehensive peace treaty with Israel, guaranteeing national security, providing generous financial assistance, and cementing his position as a champion and protector of the Jewish people. This treaty marks the beginning of the Tribulation, a seven-year period of God's judgments on the world, as described in the book of Revelation. It culminates in the Battle of Armageddon and ultimately leads to the return of the true Messiah.

While Evangelical Christians refer to this figure as the Antichrist, this name is only mentioned once in the New Testament. In fact, there are over 30 titles for the False Messiah in both the Old and New Testament.

Ps.   5-6 The Bloody and Deceitful Man
Ps. 10:2-4 The Wicked One
Ps. 10:18 The Man of the Earth
Ps. 52:1   The Mighty Man
Ps. 53:3   The Enemy
Ps. 74:8-10 The Adversary
Ps. 111:6 The Head of Many Countries
Ps. 140:1 The Violent Man
Is. 10:5-12   The Assyrian
Is. 14:2   The King of Babylon
Is. 14:12 The Sun of the Morning
Is. 16:4-5; Jer. 6:26   The Spoiler
Is. 22:25   The Nail
Is. 25:5 The Branch of the Terrible Ones
Ezek. 21:25-27   The Profane Wicked
Prince of Israel
Dan. 7:8   The Little Horn
Dan. 9:26 The Prince That Shall Come
Dan. 11:121   The Vile Person
Dan. 11:36   The Willful King
Zech. 11:16-17   The Idol Shepherd
2 Thess. 2:3   The Man of Sin
2 Thess. 2:3   The Son of Perdition
2 Thess. 2:8   The Lawless One
Rev. 9:11   The Angel of the Bottomless Pit
John 5:43   Another Coming in His Own
Name
Dan. 8:23 The King of Fierce Countenance

Matt. 24:1 The Abomination of
Desolation
Dan. 9:27 The Desolator
Ezek. 28:12 The King of Tyre
Jer. 4:6-7 The Lion
Jer. 4:6-7 The destroyer of the nations
Is.   14:12 Lucifer

Daniel chapter 9 predicts the destruction of the Second Temple. Daniel 9:26 states that it is destroyed by the people of the "prince that shall come," who rises out of the Revived Roman Empire:

"And after the sixty-two weeks
Messiah shall be cut off, but not for Himself;
And the people of the prince who is to come
Shall destroy the city and the sanctuary.
The end of it shall be with a flood,
And till the end of the war desolations are
determined.

Moreover, the passage provides the seven-year time frame of the unholy covenant: *Then he shall confirm the covenant with many for one week."* *(Daniel 9:27).*

Abomination of Desolation

From this verse the Scripture predicts the event Jesus referenced twice in the Gospels: The Abomination of Desolation. This topic is discussed in detail in a later chapter.

"But in the middle of the week, He will put an end to sacrifice and offering. And on the wing of abominations shall be one who makes desolate, even until the consummation, which is determined, is poured out on the desolate." (Daniel 9:27)

Daniel 12:11 provides further insight, specifying the number of days: *"And from the time that the daily sacrifice is taken away, and the Abomination of Desolation is set up, there shall be one thousand two hundred and ninety days."*

Same Passages from the Tanakh

The Tanakh (Jewish Bible) records the same passage in Daniel 12:11:

"And from the time the daily sacrifice was removed and the silent abomination placed, there will be one thousand, two hundred, and ninety [days]."

In the Tanakh, Daniel 9:27 is written differently, yet still references the covenant for one week. Moreover, it confirms that in the middle of the week, the abomination occurs and the sacrifices come to an end. It states:

And he will strengthen a covenant for the princes for one week, and half the week he will abolish sacrifice and meal- offering, and on high, among abominations, will be the dumb one, and until destruction and extermination befall the dumb one.

Note that the Jewish Bible uses the term "dumb" or "silent" to describe the abomination of desolation, as seen in both Daniel 9:27 and 12:11.

The Treaty's Time Frame

This passage is remarkable for its specificity regarding the peace treaty's duration: a week, equivalent to seven years. Notably, the treaty is breached at the midpoint of this seven-year term.

Despite Evangelicals' familiarity with this concept, the covenant's full implications have remained largely unexplored. Furthermore, the treaty itself has received scant attention beyond superficial analyses. As a result, widespread misconceptions and misinformation persist.

Hal Lindsey's bestselling book, "The Late Great Planet Earth," made some remarkable predictions about the end times. He accurately identified the European Community as the precursor to the Revived Roman Empire, which would give rise to the False Messiah [1]. Lindsey also correctly forecasted the decline of the United States as a global power back in 1970.

However, Lindsey's speculation about the peace treaty was off the mark. He believed it would be brokered by Arab nations, deceiving Israel into a false sense of security. Despite this error, Evangelicals have mistakenly hailed every peace initiative since Camp David as "the peace treaty," including the recent Abraham Accords.

Unfortunately, this misunderstanding has led Evangelicals far astray from the actual Treaty referenced in the Bible.

The Covenant

The fact that Scripture refers to the treaty as "the covenant" underscores its significance in God's purpose. Similarly, the Abrahamic Covenant is often preceded by "the," signifying its uniqueness, exclusivity, and divine origin. This covenant holds immense importance in God's plan for humanity.

The False Messiah's promise bearing the same title, "the covenant," reveals two key aspects:

1. This unholy agreement plays a significant role in God's plan.
2. It is a counterfeit of God's covenant with His people.

This distinction establishes that the treaty is more than a routine political agreement or ordinary peace accord. Its designation as "the covenant" reveals its profound spiritual implications.

The remainder of this book will provide the details of this unholy covenant. It will connect the dots from the Scriptures, Jewish and Evangelical teachings and the writings of the early church fathers and from Christ Himself.

2 COVENANT WITH DEATH

Isaiah 28:14-19 elaborates on the treaty, referring to it as a "covenant with death" and an "agreement with hell." This passage also reiterates that this accord will be broken.

Notably, this arrangement is distinct from any events during ancient Israel's kingdom period. For instance, the Roman-Jewish treaty between Judas Maccabeus and the Roman Republic during the Maccabee period was a deed of friendship, vastly different from the covenant described in Scripture.

Therefore, hear the word of the Lord, you scornful men,
Who rule this people who are in Jerusalem,
15 Because you have said, "We have made a

covenant with death,
   And with Sheol we are in agreement.
   When the overflowing scourge passes through,
   It will not come to us,
   For we have made lies our refuge,
   And under falsehood we have hidden ourselves."
16 Therefore thus says the Lord God:
"Behold, I lay in Zion a stone for a foundation,
A tried stone, a precious cornerstone, a sure
foundation.
Whoever believes will not act hastily.
17 Also I will make justice the measuring line,
And righteousness the plummet.
The hail will sweep away the refuge of lies,
And the waters will overflow the hiding place.
18 Your covenant with death will be annulled,
And your agreement with Sheol will not stand.
When the overflowing scourge passes through,
Then you will be trampled down by it.
19 As often as it goes out it will take you.
For morning by morning, it will pass over,
And by day and by night.
It will be a terror just to understand the report."

In Isaiah 28:18, God describes the peace treaty that initiates the tribulation as a "covenant with death" and an "agreement with hell." The Bible provides several passages that offer details about this covenant, along with less direct references that offer glimpses into its significance [1]. This treaty is more than just a peace agreement; its designation as a "covenant" underscores its importance. The Abrahamic covenant comes to mind, highlighting the spiritual implications of this evil covenant.

The Bible's emphasis on this covenant suggests it's more than a standard peace treaty. Some believe the European Union may be the revived Roman Empire, launching the False Messiah, or Antichrist, and providing his political seat. If so, it's logical that this evil treaty would emerge from the Union through the Antichrist [1].

Key Points to Consider:

- **The Covenant's Significance:** Its designation as a "covenant" emphasizes its importance.
- **Biblical Context:** The Abrahamic covenant provides a spiritual framework for understanding this evil covenant.
- **Prophetic Interpretations:** Some see the European Union as the revived Roman Empire, tied to the Antichrist's rise.

Death a Principality

The treaty's reference to a "covenant with Death" signifies that it is made with Satan himself and his demonic hierarchy, ushering in both physical and spiritual extermination. Death, the highest principality under Satan, entered the world immediately after humanity's fall.

In Genesis 2:17, God warns Adam: "but of the tree of the knowledge of good and evil you shall not eat, for in the day that you eat of it you shall surely die." The Hebrew word for "die" here signifies actual loss of life. Moreover, Adam and Eve experienced spiritual death, separating them from God.

Genesis 2:9 describes two pivotal trees in Eden, both planted by God: "the tree of life" and "the tree of the knowledge of good and evil." Notably, the tree is described as knowing "evil" because, until Adam and Eve ate the fruit, they knew only God's goodness, unaware of evil's existence.

In Eden, two trees stood: one offering eternal life and the other, death. However, death encompassed more than mere physical decay; it represented a realm and domain that included Hades. This introduces Death and Hades, chief principalities and powers directly under Satan's authority.

In Revelation, Death and Hades are tasked with orchestrating widespread mortality. Ultimately, they are cast into the lake of fire. The Covenant with Death and the Agreement with Hell (Hades) entrusts them with overseeing the demise of Israel's children—a tragic event unfolding under the Antichrist's reign.

Essentially, this covenant involves the unholy trinity of Satan and his two most powerful minions, Death and Hades. This sinister alliance ensures the devastating consequences of this pact.

Lies Our Refuge

We see clearly that the False Messiah or Antichrist who makes the covenant breaks it. Moreover, God cites the Jews who embrace the agreement as a refuge, saying, "for we have made lies our refuge." In my book on the Ezekiel 38 war, God makes it very clear to the nation of Israel that He is back. The righteous Jews at that time will not embrace this covenant; instead, the God of Israel is their refuge. These righteous Jews will include the 144,000 who will rise from Israel's Haredim. For more information, see my book, "The 144 Thousand of Revelation Explained and Identified, Israel's Haredim." We also glimpse that, rather than looking to the God of Israel, the unrighteous Jews look to this treaty and its leader.

According to biblical prophecy, the 144,000 are believed to be sealed and protected by God, consisting of 12,000 from each of the 12 tribes of Israel [1]. They are considered "firstfruits" to God and the Lamb, representing the first among the Jews to turn their hearts to Christ during the Tribulation [2]. This group is seen as a remnant of Israel who remain faithful to God, while others may follow the Antichrist.

3 THE UNHOLY COVENANT

The covenant is an unholy covenant that will dare to imitate the Abrahamic Covenant. This aligns with the Antichrist's aims and actions. Satan blasphemes and mimics the Godhead; it stands to reason he will also tread on the Abrahamic Covenant with his version.

Ezekiel 13-A Counterfeit

In Ezekiel, chapter 13, we find the next mention. This passage pertains to Ezekiel's days and the numerous false prophets of that time. Verse 10 references hailstones destroying the wall, also seen in Isaiah. Great hailstones are among Revelation's plagues – 100-pound hail (Revelation 16:21). God is angry with prophets and prophetesses speaking from their hearts, promising the Israelites peace. Verse 16 reads:

"That is, the prophets of Israel who prophesy concerning Jerusalem, and who see visions of peace for her, when there is no peace, says the Lord God."

God knows what is coming. We also see something else in chapter 13, a reference to the wall of untampered mortar.

10 "Because, indeed, because they have seduced My people, saying, 'Peace!' when there is no peace—and one builds a wall, and they plaster it with untempered mortar—

11 say to those who plaster it with untempered mortar, that it will fall. There will be flooding rain, and you, O great hailstones, shall fall; and a stormy wind shall tear it down.

12 Surely, when the wall has fallen, will it not be said to you, 'Where is the mortar with which you plastered it?'"

13 Therefore thus says the Lord God: "I will cause a stormy wind to break forth in My fury; and there shall be a flooding rain in My anger, and great hailstones in fury to consume it.

14 So I will break down the wall you have plastered with untempered mortar, and bring it down to the ground, so that its foundation will be uncovered; it will fall, and you shall be consumed in the midst of it. Then you shall know that I am the Lord.

15 "Thus will I accomplish My wrath on the wall and on those who have plastered it with untempered mortar; and I will say to you, 'The wall is no more, nor those who plastered it,

16 that is, the prophets of Israel who prophesy concerning Jerusalem, and who see visions of peace for her when there is no peace,'" says the Lord God.

Biblical Counterfeits

This isn't the only place we see counterfeits in the Bible. In the account of Babel, we see the tower made with bricks in Genesis 11:3:

3 Then they said to one another, "Come, let us make bricks and bake them thoroughly." They had brick for stone, and they had asphalt for mortar.

This was the builders' attempt to be like God. All they can offer is a counterfeit, extending from Babel to Babylon, represented by the Whore of Babylon in Revelation 17 and 18. Thus, we see the wall built with untempered mortar represents false security, angering God because it counterfeits His.

Thus, we see the wall built with untempered mortar represents false security, angering God because it counterfeits His.

We see in prophetic forecasts many contrasts between the False Messiah (Antichrist) and Jesus, and Satan's imitations. The wall built with tempered mortar will likely represent this covenant with Israel: just as God had a covenant with Israel, so too will the Antichrist.

Spiritual Dimension

In one passage, we learn that the covenant is confirmed by many. Moreover, it has a spiritual dimension, evidenced by references to it as a covenant with death and an agreement with hell. It is an agreement with the three chief principalities and powers: Satan (via the Antichrist), Death, and Hades. The Bible specifies that the accord offers peace to the nation. Based on scriptural details, we can speculate on the type of alliance or peace offered.

Ten Facts of the Unholy Covenant

In summary, we know ten facts about the

unholy covenant.

1. The unholy covenant is referenced six times in the Bible.

2. The book of Daniel is the first and only Old Testament book to reference the holy covenant, differentiating it from the unholy covenant.

3. The unholy covenant enlists the highest principalities and powers: Satan, Death, and Hades.

4. The unholy covenant is broken, contrasting with God's covenant, which is eternal.

5. The unholy covenant initially mimics the Abrahamic covenant.

6. The unholy covenant, like Babel, is a counterfeit, with its tempered mortar wall for Jerusalem.

7. The unholy covenant, once broken, seeks to annihilate the Jews.

8. The unholy covenant is broken when the

abomination of desolation takes place; additionally, the False Messiah, aka the Antichrist, lays siege to Jerusalem, takes possession of it, and establishes his capital there, taking it from the Jews.

9. In the aftermath of the breaking of the unholy covenant, the Antichrist declares himself God, blasphemes the Trinity, and changes times and laws.

10. The unholy covenant brings God's judgment.

The Setting for the Treaties Arrival

At the time of the False Messiah's covenant several key events have taken place. First and foremost, he is in his political seat. He heads the European Union and has taken the role of Commission President. The Ezekiel 38 war has occurred. This is the Russian coalition against Isael discussed in my book on the Ezekiel 38 war, the counterpart to this book.

Gentile Church Raptured Sealing of 144K

The Gentile church has been raptured

simultaneously with the catastrophic weather events predicted to accompany and defeat the Ezekiel 38 coalition. The removal of Gentile church individuals is seen as another devastating effect of man-made climate change. The Antichrist redirects the world's attention from God and the fulfillment of prophecy to his policies. The False Messiah garners action on climate change from leaders worldwide.

Meanwhile, the dispensation has switched to the children of Israel. The 144,000 young Jewish men have been sealed, primarily from the Haredim. They teach about God's great miracle and how the God of Israel is back. The veil is lifted from their eyes, and they also come to see the Messiah as Jesus Christ; this rivets their community and teachings.

Essentially, the Ezekiel 38 war sets the stage for the Antichrist to come out on behalf of Israel, offering them protection and security to provide the peace and safety described in Ezekiel.

It was the early church fathers, who had been under Apostle John, who stated that the Antichrist would be received as the False

Messiah.

According to Larry D. Harper, whose book "Antichrist" details the early church fathers' writings, they agreed on another point: the Antichrist will be Jewish and accepted by the Jews as the Messiah. He will rise from the tribe of Dan, as explained in my various books on the Antichrist.

Him You Will Accept

Jesus's one direct reference to the Antichrist is that he would be accepted. Jesus stated in John 5:43, "*I am coming in my Father's name, and you receive me not; if another shall come in his own name, him you will receive.*"

The Greek word for "another" denotes one besides, or one of two; with a particular article, it means "the other." Jesus is referring here to the False Messiah and to those who will receive him. This is a loaded statement, as Jesus was coming as the Messiah; He was referring to His nemesis, who would be received as such.

The verse uses the word "if," but it also means "whosoever," which provides further elaboration. The disciples of John understood that the False Messiah was coming. Jesus predicted in that statement that the nation would receive him – not the nation as a whole, as there will be a clear division between righteous and unrighteous Jews.

Today, the Antichrist, as the False Messiah, has been totally disregarded in Bible prophecy. Instead, myths proliferate. Nearly all teachers only look at the headlines of the day and make them fit. Additionally, they erroneously hail every Israel-Palestinian peace initiative as "the Antichrist's Treaty." Furthermore, they taught that Donald Trump's Abraham Accords were the Tribulation agreement. None of these fit the Antichrist's covenant of death, referenced in Isaiah 28:18, or Jesus's predictions. This passage provides a good deal of information on what to expect from the false Messiah.

Many times, in studying end-time prophecy, you must connect the dots. Moreover, you must study to know the Scriptures involved to connect them. This book will do precisely that. It will provide the details of the Antichrist's peace treaty and show why unrighteous Jews will accept him as the Messiah or a Messiah-like figure.

4 TEACHINGS ON JEWISH MESSIAH

A good hint at what will be in the treaty is what Judaism teaches about the Mashiach. What are they looking for in the Messiah, and what will be the signs of his coming? When we examine end-time Jewish beliefs, we see that they overlap with and contrast our own. Moreover, their doctrines have remained unchanged for two thousand years, except to become more clarified and specific in certain areas.

This was due in part to the work of Moses ben Maimon, known as Maimonides, or by the acronym Rambam. He lived from 1138 to 1204 and was a prolific and influential Torah scholar of the Middle Ages. He wrote the "13 Principles of Faith," which summarized the required beliefs of Judaism. These principles are still referenced by many rabbis today. One of the thirteen principles is "the belief in the arrival of the Messiah and the messianic era."

As the teachings are examined, we can see that they both cross over and overlap with Evangelical prophecy. Moreover, they are setting the stage for the Jews to accept the Antichrist as their Messiah. Going a step further, we can see that the beliefs about what Jews expect from the Messiah will be the very things that the unholy covenant will provide. We see this more clearly as we examine Jewish teachings.

2. Gog and Magog in Judaism

While Jewish teachings do not emphasize prophecy like Evangelical doctrines, one of their prophetic forecasts centers around the Gog Magog war. Whereas I teach that the Gog Magog war will usher in the Antichrist's peace treaty, Jews have another perspective on the war. They see it as the final battle between good and evil, ushering in a period of eternal peace. Again, Jewish theology does not dwell on end times like independent Bible-believing faiths. Nevertheless, in their teachings, they instruct that when Jews are living securely in

Israel, Gog will invade, and God will furiously retaliate.

According to My Jewish Learning:

"Ezekiel promises the restoration of the descendants of Jacob, the Jewish exiles will be gathered back to their land, and never again will God's face be hidden from the Jewish people.

The wars of Gog and Magog, as the prophecy came to be referred to in later sources, are part of a larger belief that the messianic age will be preceded by a period of great suffering and upheaval — the so-called "birth pangs of the Messiah." But in general, belief in the messianic age, while clearly part of Jewish belief and tradition, are not discussed in great detail in ancient rabbinic sources."

We see two similarities with Evangelical end-times teaching:

1. Both Evangelicals and Jews believe in the birth pangs.

2. Both also look to the Ezekiel 38 war.

In my book on the Ezekiel 38-39 War, I

teach that this event provides the timing of the Rapture – when the Gentile church is removed. This will occur simultaneously with the great earthquake, fire, and hail that defeat the army. Meanwhile, the 144,000 Jewish witnesses are sealed.

Jewish Teachings Not Specific on Names of Countries

While Evangelical teachings on Ezekiel 38-39 specify the various countries, Jewish teachings leave their identity more ambiguous. Although they believe the specifics are flexible, they also teach that this battle ushers in the Mashiach.

Rabbi Reuven Lauffer, from Hidabroot-Torah and Judaism, stated:

"There is a tradition that before the Messiah comes there will be a battle of Gog ...will come from the saffron from the north saffron refers to something which is unclear something which is northwards, northern countries, places that are full of darkness and evil, what the Christians call Armageddon. Its the war that will end all wars. It's the war that will herald in the Messianic era.

According to Jewish tradition, Gog and Magog will be something absolutely terrible. The repercussions will be enormous; many people will die. Through this, the Mashiach will come, enabling him to reveal his identity and redeem the Jewish people. Before that happens, it will be very dire. It will seem like everything is over.

Rabbi Mendel Kessin, from Hidabroot - Torah & Judaism, stated:

"Who is Gog and Magog is flexible. It can only happen if the Mashiach is alive at that time. It's a messianic war, it's a war after the mashiach has come…it has to be against the Jews, and it has to be with the Mashiach alive. Gog and Magog can only happen 1, if it's against the Jews and 2, if the Mashiach is alive at that time, because it's really a Messianic war, it's a war after the Mashiach has come."

Therefore, it becomes clear that the Jews are flexible regarding which nations comprise the Ezekiel 38-39 war. Nevertheless, they agree that the Messiah will be alive at that time and will be revealed. Thus, when the Antichrist, as head of the EU empire, proposes a peace treaty, the Jews will be primed to receive him.

The Birth Pangs

Another similar teaching shared by Jews and Evangelicals is the concept of birth pangs. This belief holds that times will grow increasingly evil and wicked before the coming of the Mashiach. Evangelicals instruct that these events precede the start of the Tribulation, while Jews profess that it signals the first coming of their Mashiach.

Rabbi Yirmiyahu Ullman of Hildabroot-Torah and Judaism teaches in his lecture: *"God and Magog: Characteristics of the End of Days"*

"End of Days-Period is called Armageddon. War of Gog, Magog are wars of Armageddon It is the period of the coming of Mashiach and the world to come:
The warming of the world toward the coming of Messiah…Tumultuous days coming of Messiah Cataclysmic tumultuous time (Daniel) the suffering that might be getting the world ready for the Messiah."

While Rabbi Ullman spoke about the

difficulty of the end times, he appeared to reference another leader preceding the Mashiach, which aligns with the characteristics of the Antichrist. He stated:

"Book of Daniel much worse than the Jewish people ever experienced, much worse than Egypt, or the destruction of the 1st and 2nd Temple. Much worse than the Holocaust, not going to be an easy period. A good deal of calamity. Compared to labor pains more intense and frequent getting ready for the birth of the arrival of the Mashiach when the world will be relieved of all of these tensions. Until then it will cause great pain and suffering, and people might be crying out until the birth of the redemption. Until then it will be very difficult.

When is the time, some commentators have named times past and it was not that they were wrong, it was that the Jews didn't merit the redemption."

Jewish Birth Pang Scriptures

The birth pains referenced in Jewish teachings are found in several biblical passages. Micah 4:10 states: *"For pangs have seized you like a woman in labor. Be in pain, and labor to bring forth, O daughter of Zion.*" Additionally, Isaiah 66:8 reads: "*Who has heard such a thing? Who has seen such things? Shall the earth be made to give birth in one day? Or shall a nation be born at once? For as soon as Zion was in labor, she gave birth to her children.*"

Mashiach Coming Any Second

Based on Jewish expectations and their overlap with Evangelical teachings, many Jews will likely believe the Antichrist is their Messiah or a type of Messiah. Jesus's references teach that while the Jews rejected Him, they will accept the one coming in his own name (John 5:43). Theologian Arthur Pink noted in his book on the Antichrist that the word used indicates he is also from the lineage of Abraham. Not only would the Antichrist be hailed as the Jewish Messiah, but he would also identify himself as God on earth. The False Messiah, also known as the Antichrist, is the nemesis of Lord Jesus Christ, and his coming would precede the return of the real Messiah.

According to Rabbi Alon Anava, "Mashiach is coming any second. There are sources that prove Mashiach must come now."

Rabbi Lawrence Hajioff further noted that the Mashiach will be married and have children. Hajioff provided additional details, stating that Mashiach's arrival will be imminent, and he will be married. Moreover, he must prove his descent from King David. During one of his lectures, Rabbi Hajioff taught:

'Law of Kings… Mashiach a king… Kingship is going to return to the Jewish people. Descendant of King David…He must prove and have a book goes back and proves it, many were lost in the Holocaust but such books exist…The Mashiach is going to have to prove it…Can we do something that can bring Mashiach? What we are seeing in Israel today is laying the groundwork for the coming Mashiach. More Jews have died because of false messiahs."

"Mashiach can come at any moment When Mashiach comes won't need the Jewish holidays anymore. Every moment there must be a potential Mashiach every day. Or we're so good or we're so bad Mashiach is going to come. He is going to be the greatest prophet in Jewish history except for Moshe Rabbenu."
"He is not going to be the Savior the Christian world sees him as the savior. He is not the

savior we have to save ourselves. The anointed one-to pour something on someone else. The king would inspire the people and they were the spiritual light Mashiach is going to be a man whose married whose had kids whose made mistakes, who's sinned. [We are] going to see the battle of God Magog before the Mashiach comes. He's going to complete the world…Entire world is improved through this."

We see in Jewish beliefs the concept of birth pangs and the imminent arrival of the Mashiach, especially after the Ezekiel 38-39 war. This aligns seamlessly with the idea that the Ezekiel 38 war will usher in the Antichrist's covenant. Furthermore, Jewish beliefs regarding the Mashiach's role as a king remain unchanged since the time of Christ. Jesus predicted that the Jews, as a nation, would accept the one coming in his own name (John 5:43). His prophecy has held true for 2,000 years, and it remains fulfilled, just as He foretold.

5 MESHIACH BUILDS THE THIRD TEMPLE

In addition to predicting the future, Jesus provided the first glimpse of what would be in the unholy covenant when He said that the Jews would accept the one coming in his own name as their Messiah. The early church fathers confirmed this, stating that the Antichrist would be received as the Messiah.

When examining Jewish teachings on the Messiah, one of the expected deeds on his behalf is rebuilding the Jewish temple. According to the 2,300 days of Daniel (Daniel 8:13), we know that the Temple is built seven months after the start of the seven-year unholy covenant.

The 2300 Days of Daniel

Daniel 8 14. states, "*Then I heard a holy one speaking and another holy one said to the one who spoke, 'for how long is the vision concerning the regular burnt offering, the transgression that makes desolate, and the giving over of the sanctuary and host to be trampled underfoot,*" and it reads in verse 14, " *And he said to me for 2300 evenings and mornings then the sanctuary shall be restored to its rightful state.*"

The 2,300 days have been interpreted by theologians as applying to the ancient king Antiochus Epiphanes. Got Questions provides a commentary, and their teachings are generally excellent. However, they suggest that this verse also predicts some of Antiochus Epiphanes' actions. According to Got Questions, "The time period of 2,300 days figures to approximately six and a third years. We believe the prophecy was fulfilled before the birth of Christ during the reign of the Seleucid king Antiochus IV Epiphanes."

Theologians uniformly agree that the mysterious 2,300 days of Daniel refer to a past event. However, this interpretation is incorrect. The verse actually applies to the Tribulation. As the passage reads: *"Then I heard a holy one speaking and another holy one said to the one who spoke for how long is the vision concerning the regular burnt offering, the transgression that makes desolate."*

This is the abomination of desolation, which occurs when the False Messiah enters the Holy of Holies and declares himself to be God. It continues: *" and the giving over of the sanctuary and the host to be trampled underfoot. And he said to me for 2300 evenings and mornings then the sanctuary shall be restored to its rightful state."*

Calculating the Days

The evenings and mornings constitute a day. However, the verse also states, "then the sanctuary shall be restored to its rightful state" (Daniel 8:14).

The total duration of the Tribulation is seven years, equivalent to 2,520 days (1260 + 1260). Subtracting 2,300 days from this total leaves 220 days, approximately seven months. This suggests that from the start of the Tribulation, when the False Messiah (also known as the Antichrist) signs the treaty guaranteeing Israel's peace, there will be roughly seven months before the Temple is rebuilt. The verse specifies, "For 2,300 evenings and mornings, then the sanctuary shall be restored to its rightful state" (Daniel 8:14). This provides a strong hint that the False Messiah, or Antichrist, will facilitate the Temple's rebuilding through the treaty.

Seven Months Temple Completed

Seven months after the start of the Tribulation, the Temple will be completed. This is essentially what the verse is conveying. From the time the Temple is completed and sacrifices begin, there will be 2,300 evenings and mornings until the end of the Tribulation. After 1,050 days, the sacrifices will cease, marking the 1,260th day. For the final three and a half years, there will be no sacrifices. The False Messiah, also known as the Antichrist, will declare the Temple as his own.

Let's examine the verse in light of this understanding:

"Then I heard a holy one speaking, and another holy one said to the one who spoke, 'For how long is the vision concerning the regular burnt offering, the transgression that makes desolate?'" (Daniel 8:13).

This verse encompasses the period from the start of the first burnt offering to the transgression that makes desolate - the abomination of desolation and the surrender of the sanctuary and its host to be trampled underfoot. This signifies the final three and a half years, during which the Antichrist will seize control of the Temple, lay siege to Israel, and persecute the Jews.

The Temple Returns to Its Rightful State

The verse continues: "And he said to me, 'For 2,300 evenings and mornings, then shall the sanctuary be restored to its rightful state'" (Daniel 8:14). The "rightful state" refers to the period when the real Messiah, Jesus Christ, returns. At that time, the Temple initiated by the Antichrist will be destroyed, making way for God's Temple described in Revelation.

This verse is simpler than theologians often suggest. It describes the Tribulation period, specifically what happens at the 2,300-day mark, when the Temple is completed and sacrifices begin. The verse also indicates that by the end of the Tribulation, the Temple will return to its rightful state.

The construction of the Third Temple is initiated by the Antichrist through his false covenant of peace. However, he will desecrate the Temple, committing the abomination of desolation, and more. Ultimately, the verse assures us that the Temple will return to its rightful state.

One can only imagine the immense deception that the Jewish people will face when this leader offers to rebuild the Temple, finance it, and secure it for them. The deception will be so profound and persuasive that only through God Himself providing the wisdom and understanding mentioned in the prophetic books will some be able to resist. Specifically, young men from the Haredim community will receive this revelation and will instruct others.

The Seven Month Accuracy To Build

According to Chabad.org, the Third Temple is estimated to measure approximately 22,325,625 square feet. (link unavailable) notes that most commercial buildings over 10,000 square feet typically require 4-6 months to construct. Larger, more complex structures, such as office buildings and industrial facilities exceeding 50,000 square feet, often take 6-8 months. Therefore, the predicted seven-month construction period for the Temple aligns with modern building methods.

Notably, Solomon's Temple took seven years to build, whereas modern technology reduces this timeframe to just seven months. The Book of Daniel's prediction of this exact timeframe is truly remarkable, especially considering its ancient origins.

Destruction of Al-Aqsa Mosque Change of World Opinion

The Ezekiel 38-39 war will destroy the Al-Aqsa Mosque through the massive earthquake predicted in the passage. Since the coalition includes Muslim nations, this invasion will instantly spark anti-Muslim sentiment, similar to the backlash following Russia's invasion of Ukraine. Imagine the global impact of a surprise attack on this scale. The Russian-Ukrainian conflict may have taught Russia the importance of surrounding a nation beforehand to ensure preparedness. However, in Ukraine's case, Russia was waiting for NATO concessions that never materialized. Nonetheless, this set a precedent for unified global condemnation and anti-Russia sentiment in Western nations.

This precedent could pave the way for the False Messiah, also known as the Antichrist, to publicly support the Jewish people and Israel after the Ezekiel war.

The EU: The Leading Power

At the time of this war, the European Union will emerge as a powerful empire, with the euro serving as the world's leading reserve currency. The US will have declined, struggling with a dollar crisis. Europe, however, will not yet have reached its pinnacle of power. This occurs during the first three and a half years of the seven-year period, as described in Daniel's prophecy of the little horn rising to power. Daniel also notes that the leader will work deceitfully.

After consolidating power, his empire will reach its height of strength, particularly at the abomination of desolation. (More information on this topic can be found in my other books.)

Just as the EU defended Ukraine, it will also intervene on behalf of Israel, now led by the man many will regard as the Mashiach. Following God's defeat of the great army, he will emerge as the leader, facilitating the Temple's rebuilding through his covenant, providing funding, authority, and means.

Provision in Treaty for Rebuilding Temple

Rabbi Skobak, in his lecture "A Third Holy Temple? What Does Judaism Teach about the Rebuilt 3rd Temple in Jerusalem?" states: "Do we have to wait for the Messiah to build the Temple, or can we begin its construction prior to his coming?... numerous views exist on this question in the Talmud, Rasheim, and Maimonides' writings."

Maimonides suggests that if the Temple remains unbuilt when the Messiah arrives, he will build it, proving his authenticity. Others argue that construction can begin before the Messiah's coming. Leading Torah scholars believe the people of Israel can rebuild the Temple without waiting.

The unholy covenant will likely provide for the rebuilding of the Third Temple, guaranteeing funding and ensuring that only the Jewish Temple can be built on the site.

False Messiah's Temple

In 2 Samuel 7:12-13, God states that the Messiah's descendant will build a house for His name, establishing the throne of his kingdom forever. The Antichrist's Temple, however, is built in defiance of the God of Israel, desecrated and claimed as his own. This will deceive many Jews, as Maimonides predicted.

6 RETURN JEWS TO ISRAEL AND RECOGNIZE TORAH

Another feature of the False Messiah's covenant is that he will bring the remaining Jews back to Israel and recognize the Torah as Israel's law.

According to Mia Anderssén-Löf's article, "May He Speedily Come: The role of the Messiah in Haredi and Hardal Judaism":

"The messiah will be recognized by the fact that he will be a Jewish leader who brings all Jews to repent and follow the laws of the Torah. Once he does this, it may be safely assumed that he is the messiah. Once the entire Jewish and non-Jewish world has recognized him as the messiah, his next task will be to bring back the Jewish exiles and build the Temple. If he does this, then he is certainly the messiah. If he fails at this second stage or dies before completing it, then he is not the messiah." (JAZ 2015d)

Jews for Judaism provides details on the actions of the Mashiach:

1. He will ingather all Jews back to Israel from the 2000-year exile to live in their homeland (Deuteronomy 30:3, Isaiah 11:11-12, Jeremiah 30:3, 32:37, Ezekiel 11:17, 36:24).
2. He will rebuild the Holy Temple.
3. He will establish worldwide peace, disarmament, and an end to war (Micah 4:1-4, Hosea 2:20, Isaiah 2:1-4, 60:18).
4. He will reign at a time when all Jews embrace the Torah and follow its commandments.
5. He will come at a time when all people recognize the one true God of Abraham, Isaac, and Jacob.

The Mashiach must be a member of the tribe of Judah and a direct descendant of King David and Solomon (Numbers 1:1-18).

[He] will descend from kings David and

Solomon, be wise and righteous, and be the anointed king of Israel. The Jewish exiles will return to Israel, national repentance will occur among God's people, the Temple will be restored, Jews will live in peace, nations will turn to the God of Israel, and knowledge of God will fill the world.

An interesting footnote is that the Mashiach will usher in worldwide peace and disarmament, an ideology also found in Catholic teachings and the European Union's foundation.

We can conclude that the Treaty's provisions will allow the Torah to be Israel's law and provide funding for Jews to return to Israel. The Antichrist may offer funding for a year, flights, and moving expenses reimbursed.

When Emmanuel Macron became president of France, newspapers hailed him as Jupiter, a mythological god comparable to God. Similar headlines will accompany the False Messiah, also known as the Antichrist, as the Mashiach.

The Antichrist's peace treaty, forecast to begin the Tribulation, will mimic the Abrahamic covenant, promising Israel peace, safety, and military and financial support.

The Ezekiel 38-39 war will give the Antichrist the opportunity to aid Israel, taking a stand despite the two-state solution policy.

The False Messiah's aid and promise of peace and prosperity will gain him Jewish favor. When they learn of his Jewish ancestry and proposals, they will hail him as the Messiah.

At that time, there will be two types of Jews in Israel: the righteous and unrighteous, those who accept the False Messiah and those who recognize his true identity, thanks to the 144 Jewish Servants.

The Covenant of Death

In Isaiah 28:18, God refers to the Treaty as a "*covenant with death*" and an "*agreement with hell.*" Ezekiel 13:16 states:

"That is, the prophets of Israel who prophesy concerning Jerusalem and see visions of peace for her when there is no peace, says the Lord God."

Psalm 55:20-21 describes the False

Messiah's aims:

"He has put forth his hands against those who were at peace with him: he has broken his covenant. The words of his mouth were smoother than butter, but war was in his heart: his words were softer than oil, yet they were drawn swords."

Isaiah 33:7-9 adds:

"Surely their valiant ones shall cry outside, the ambassadors of peace shall weep bitterly. The highways lie waste, the wayfaring man ceases. He has broken the covenant, He has despised the cities He regards no man.

7 CURRENT AFFAIRS & THE FUTURE TREATY

Currently, Evangelical prophecy pundits are examining every war and conflict surrounding Israel, as well as all peace initiatives, as the Antichrist's treaty. However, it is actually these ambitions that contribute to peace, setting the stage for the Ezekiel 38 attack.

Ezekiel 38: 8-11 describes this peace in the following verses:

8 After many days you will be visited. In the latter years, you will come into the land of those brought back from the sword and gathered from many people on the mountains of Israel, which had long been desolate; they were brought out of the nations, and now all of them dwell safely. 9 You will ascend, coming like a storm, covering the land like a cloud, you and all your troops and many peoples with you."

10 'Thus says the Lord God: "On that day it shall come to pass that thoughts will arise in your mind, and you will make an evil plan: 11 You will say, 'I will go up against a land of unwalled villages; I will go to a peaceful people, who dwell safely, all of them dwelling without walls, and having neither bars nor gates."

It is clear from the passage that Israel dwells safely. The absence of 'bars nor gates' indicates that the land is not preparing for an invasion because it feels relatively at peace. This does not describe Israel today, with its conflict with Iran. However, based on this forecast, we can expect to see the issues between Iran and Israel resolved. This means no funding to Hamas and some resolution between Hamas and Israel.

Two-State Solution

Furthermore, we can expect a shift in EU Israel policy away from a two-state solution, which is the EU's current position. This shift is in preparation for the coming treaty that will be spearheaded by the False Messiah. Hugh Lovatt, Senior Policy Fellow at the European Council on Foreign Relations, wrote in his article, "The end of Oslo: A new European strategy on Israel-Palestine" (December 9, 2020):

"But, faced with Israel's consolidation of a one-state reality, public attitudes on both sides trending in opposite directions, and a shift in the political priorities of Arab states, the EU must at least acknowledge that it needs to adapt its strategy…. If it becomes apparent that it is already too late to sustain a viable and sovereign Palestinian state, the two parties will need to work out how they can live with each other as equals, preparing for a just one-state solution that provides meaningful stability and security to all."

"At the same time, Europeans must make clear that if Israel continues blocking a two-state solution, the only other acceptable means of ensuring equal rights will be through a single democratic state… A European strategy centered on equality and deoccupation, rather than negotiations and the Oslo framework, is compatible with both a one-state and a two-state paradigm."

The EU's special representative for the Middle East Peace Process, Susanna Terstal, also outlined the options: "There is only one alternative [to two states], that is one state… where two people live side by side with equal rights in peace and security."

We can expect to see a one-state solution becoming more prominent as the days move ahead toward the Ezekiel 38-39 war.

The Agreement and Three-Year Action Plan

Currently, the European Union has a treaty that serves as the basis for the future covenant: the EU-Israel Association Agreement, which entered into force in June 2000. This agreement provides a legal and institutional framework for political dialogue and economic cooperation.

The EU is Israel's largest trade market, accounting for about a third of Israel's total trade. Israel is the EU's most important trading partner in the Mediterranean area and was ranked as the EU's 24th trade partner globally in 2016. The most traded goods include chemicals and related products, machinery and transport equipment, and manufactured goods.

Israel is an Associated State of the European

Union, meeting the economic and political requirements known as the Copenhagen criteria. These criteria require a democratic, free-market government with corresponding freedoms and institutions and respect for the rule of law.

The agreement with Israel is part of the European Neighborhood Policy (ENP), a foreign relations instrument connecting countries to the east and south of EU territory. Some of these countries seek to become EU members. The EU offers financial assistance to these countries if they meet strict government and economic reform conditions.

The process is supported by an Action Plan, offering tariff-free access to EU markets and financial or technical assistance in exchange. The countries covered include Algeria, Morocco, Egypt, Israel, Jordan, Lebanon, Libya, Palestine, Syria, Tunisia in the South; and Armenia, Azerbaijan, Belarus, Georgia, Moldova, and Ukraine in the East.

Israel is also a full partner in the Horizon 2020 Research Programme, benefiting from projects worth close to €170 million per year between 2017-2020. Since December 2021,

Israel has participated in the Horizon Europe Programme.

Therefore, this association agreement, which already exists with Israel, provides the basis for the False Prophet's, also known as the Antichrist's, treaty.

The EU Delegation to Israel

In addition to the Association Agreement between the European Union and Israel, the EU also has a Delegation to Israel. Its purpose is multifaceted:

- **Representing the EU**: to represent the European Union in Israel and present the EU's positions and interests to the Government of Israel, with the overall goal of advancing relations between the EU and Israel.
- **Political Field**: to represent the EU's position with senior Israeli decision-makers and report on political events in Israel to the EU headquarters in Brussels.
- **Economic and Trade**: to maintain regular contact with government ministries and economic operators,

promoting smooth trade links between the EU and Israel.

- **Projects**: to coordinate numerous programs and projects with Israeli government ministries and civil society in Israel.
- **Public Diplomacy**: to disseminate information and respond to questions on the EU and EU-Israel relations.
- **Research and Innovation**: to help implement EU-Israel agreements and promote cooperation between Israeli and European organizations.
-

The European Parliament's Delegation for relations with Israel strengthens the bilateral relationship with the Knesset, Israel's parliament. This delegation works closely with various European Parliament bodies, including the Committee on Foreign Affairs and the Committees on International Trade and Industry, Research, and Energy.

According to the Delegation's website, Israel is a key strategic ally of the European Union, sharing values and heritage. The EU-Israel Association Agreement is based on respect for human rights and democratic principles. Israel is being integrated into European policies and programs through the European Neighborhood Policy Action Plan.

The Delegation aims to enhance relations with Israel and the wider region through parliamentary diplomacy, striving for peace, security, and stability. It contests any amalgamation between Israel's government policies and Judaism or people of Jewish origin and fights against antisemitism.

Given the existing association agreement and established Delegations to Israel with key contacts and regular dialogue, the foundation for the False Messiah's, or Antichrist's, peace treaty is already laid

8 THE FALSE MESSIAH'S TREATY

The EU Commission prepares, negotiates, and proposes the EU's agreements. Consequently, the False Messiah, as head of the Commission, can easily propose this policy. Geopolitically, the pieces are in place for the Antichrist to emerge and negotiate the treaty for Israel and the Jews, with all necessary people contacts already established.

Manfred Kohler, a regulatory expert at the European Commission and founder of the Regulatory Institute, proposed in February 2020 that new membership forms could solve EU challenges. His proposal includes various types of associate membership with variable geometry, allowing countries to opt in or out of specific EU policies. Countries like Canada could serve as a bridge between the EU and their region.

This development is alarming, as it would grant the EU unprecedented global influence by adding numerous countries. In the context of the Unholy Covenant, the Antichrist could fast-track a treaty providing Israel with EU membership protections without the need for formal membership. Israel has already fulfilled the Copenhagen Criteria, clearing the first hurdle to membership.

Recently, the EU rejected Ukraine's fast-track membership bid at the Versailles Summit, advising them to follow regular procedures. However, within a month, EU Commission President Ursula von der Leyen and an EU delegation met with President Zelenskyy, offering paperwork to expedite membership – a first in EU history.

The Details of the Unholy Covenant

The False Messiah, or Antichrist, is expected to add the following provisions to the agreement:

- **Upgraded Association Agreement**: placing Israel on par with EU membership or fast-tracking its membership under the EU's security

umbrella
- **Joint Military**: providing Israel with its own military and bolstering security forces
- **Recognition of Torah**: acknowledging Torah in the land of Israel
- **Right of Return**: providing funds for Jews outside Israel to travel, move, and settle in Israel for up to one year
- **Third Temple Funding**: securing the site as a holy place for the Jewish people
- **Seven-Year Plan**: a seven-year timeframe for funding and building assistance to rebuild and recover from invasion and earthquake
-

The Seven Month and Seven Year Coincidence

The seven-year timeframe is mentioned in Ezekiel concerning the war, where it takes seven months to clean bodies and rebuild the Temple. This parallel will likely deceive many Jews, but those with divine wisdom will see through it. Isaiah 33:6-9 confirms the broken treaty's context.

Wisdom and knowledge will be the stability of your times,

And the strength of salvation;
The fear of the Lord is His treasure.
7 Surely their valiant ones shall cry outside,
The ambassadors of peace shall weep bitterly.
8 The highways lie waste,
The traveling man ceases.
He has broken the covenant,
[b]He has despised the [c]cities,
He regards no man.
9 The earth mourns and languishes,
Lebanon is shamed and shriveled;
Sharon is like a wilderness,
And Bashan and Carmel shake off their fruits.

9 THE ABOMINATION OF DESOLATION

The Abomination of Desolation: Matthew 24:15, Mark 13:14, Daniel 8:11-14, 12:11-13, 9:26, 11:31, Joel 1:6

Within Solomon's Temple, the "most holy place" (1 Kings 6:16-36) housed the Ark of the Covenant. This sanctuary was where God dwelt among the Israelites (Exodus 25). The Ark, made of shittim wood overlaid with gold, contained the two tablets of the Ten Commandments, Aaron's rod, and manna. The sprinkled blood of sacrificed animals on the Ark's mercy seat atoned for all of Israel, symbolizing the blood of Jesus Christ, which would one day be shed to remit the world's sins. The priests followed detailed rituals of dress, conduct, and worship. When performing these rituals, God met with the Israelites and sanctified the Temple with His glory (Exodus 29:43). These details and acts symbolized the coming Messiah, who would be the propitiation for sin. In the most holy place, God reaffirmed His promise to His people.

The Abomination of Desolation

The Temple is sacred in Judaism and the most sacred place for Jewish worship. Three and a half years after the Antichrist makes his unholy covenant with Israel, he invades Jerusalem with an army (Joel 1:6, Daniel 11:31, 9:26). He then enters the most holy place, sits in the Temple, and declares himself a god (2 Thessalonians 2:4). The Antichrist terminates worship and sacrifice, committing sacrilegious acts that desecrate the Temple.

He places an abominable object in the Holy Place. His true character is revealed as he lays siege to Israel, occupies its territory, and wages war against the Jews, seeking their annihilation (Daniel 11:33-35, 12:10, Revelation 6:10-11, Jeremiah 50:33, Joel 1:6, Matthew 24:9, Mark 13:9-13).

Concurrently, he and his federation of kings abolish the Catholic Church and destroy the Vatican (Revelation 11). The False Messiah, or Antichrist, will not tolerate any religion other than the worship of, and devotion to, himself and his empire. Daniel 11:37 affirms that the Antichrist has no regard for human life or suffering.

Christ's Warning

Christ solemnly warns the Jews in Judea at that time to flee to the mountains. He commands them to run, leaving their jackets behind. He notes the additional suffering for pregnant and nursing mothers who must flee. In Matthew 24:21, Christ declares:

: *"For then there will be great Tribulation, such as has not been since the beginning of the world until this time, no, nor ever shall be."*

The Covenant of Death

In Isaiah 28:18, God refers to the treaty as a "covenant with death," an "agreement with hell." In Ezekiel chapter 13, God is angry at the prophets and prophetesses who speak from their hearts and tell the Israelites of peace.

Verse 16 reads: *"That is, the prophets of Israel who prophesy concerning Jerusalem, and who see visions of peace for her, when there is no peace, says the Lord God."* Psalm 55:20-21 describes the Antichrist's aims by stating:

"He has put forth his hands against those who were at peace with him: he has broken his covenant. The words of his mouth were smoother than butter, but war was in his heart: his words were softer than oil, yet they were drawn swords." Isaiah 33:7-9 adds: *"Surely their valiant ones shall cry outside, the ambassadors of peace shall weep bitterly. The highways lie waste, the wayfaring man ceases. He has broken the covenant, He has despised the cities He regards no man."*

Abomination of Desolation-Blasphemy of the Holy Spirit

The unique phrase "abomination of desolation" is used numerous times by Jesus as a warning. It was foretold by the prophet Daniel as the moment when the Antichrist declares himself God and sets up his technological counterpart to the Trinity in the Holy of Holies. Daniel also refers to it in Daniel 8:13 as *"the transgression of desolation."*

The verse in its entirety reads: *"Then I heard*

a saint speaking and another saint said unto that certain saint which spoke, How long shall be the vision concerning the daily sacrifice and the transgression of desolation to give both the sanctuary and the host to be trodden under foot?"

It is possible that the "transgression of desolation" is blasphemy against the Holy Spirit, a sin so grievous that it even nullifies the healing and cleansing power of Jesus Christ's blood. Satan knows this fact, which is why it's part of his reign on earth. His mark guarantees him the person's soul, leaving them without hope of redemption.

The reason for this is that the Holy Spirit plays a crucial role in the redemption process and is so holy that when blasphemed, it cannot continue its work. Instead, it must retreat to preserve its own glory, which is part of God's glory.

Revelation 13:6 tells us that the Antichrist blasphemes God, stating:

"Then he opened his mouth in blasphemy against God, to blaspheme His name, His tabernacle, and those who dwell in heaven." Consistent with his actions, the Antichrist introduces the mark of

the Beast, thereby blaspheming the Holy Spirit. This mark leads individuals to commit the unforgivable sin of blasphemy against the Holy Spirit, a topic I explore in "Decoding 666: The Number of the Beast."

Historical scholars have linked the "abomination of desolation" to Antiochus IV Epiphanes' desecration of the Second Temple, where he installed a Zeus statue. Ezekiel 6-9 describes the Israelites' idolatrous acts within the Temple, prompting God's judgment. Nevertheless, Daniel's "transgression of desolation" (Daniel 8:13) implies a more profound sacrilege. As Daniel 9:27 reveals:

27 Then he shall confirm a covenant with many for one week;
But in the middle of the week
He shall bring an end to sacrifice and offering.
And on the wing of abominations shall be one who makes desolate,
Even until the consummation, which is determined,
Is poured out on the desolate."

The word for "desolate" is a term that means to be put to silence, laid waste, or reduced to ruins. It also conveys the idea of astonishing or stunning something. This desolation is both literal and spiritual.

The "abomination of desolation" is a term that speaks not only of a literal desolation due to Jerusalem's siege but also of a spiritual one, resulting from the Holy Spirit's retreat from the Third Temple and the lives of those who take the mark of the Beast.

Since the Holy Spirit is omnipresent alongside God, in the area of the Third Temple, it will have to withdraw for the sake of its own glory.

10 THE 1260-1290 DAYS OF DANIEL

Within the books of Daniel and Revelation, we learn about the 1,260 days of persecution and death of the righteous Jews, also known as saints. We also see a parallel between those with wisdom and understanding who are able to count the number of the beast. This phrase is used in the book of Daniel to describe their plight and victory, which is recorded in Revelation.

Additionally, Daniel's 10-day testing period parallels the 10 days of Tribulation mentioned in Revelation 2:10. The two books complement each other, providing additional details on various topics, such as the beast's 10-king division, Daniel's four beasts, and Revelation's single beast. Furthermore, Revelation 12:7-9 records the war in heaven:

7: And war broke out in heaven: Michael and his angels fought with the dragon; and the dragon and his angels fought,

8 but they did not prevail, nor was a place found for them in heaven any longer.

9 So the great dragon was cast out, that serpent of old, called the Devil and Satan, who deceives the whole world; he was cast to the earth, and his angels were cast out with him.

In parallel Daniel 12:12 records:

At that time Michael shall stand up,
The great prince who stands watch over the sons of your people.
And there shall be a time of trouble,
Such as never was since there was a nation,
Even to that time.
And at that time your people shall be delivered,
Everyone who is found written in the book.

These examples illustrate the connection. Moreover, Daniel offers additional verses specifically relevant to the 144,000 anointed servants in Revelation. A common theme runs through both Daniel and Revelation.

Daniel 11: 35 states:

And some of those of understanding, (remember we see this word in Revelation for the riddle and mark of the beast) shall fall to refine them, purify them and make them white until the time of the end.

Daniel 12:10

Many shall be purified, made white, and refined but the wicked shall do wickedly; and none of the wicked shall understand but the wise shall understand. (From here a time frame is given, the next verse begins, *'From the time that the daily sacrifices is taken away and the abomination is set up, there shall be one thousand two hundred and ninety days.*

Jesus' statement, "they will deliver you up to tribulation and kill you," may allude to Revelation 2:10's ten days of tribulation, suggesting a process of suffering, possibly including torture, before martyrdom. Jesus encourages perseverance in Revelation 2:10, saying, "Be faithful until death, and I will give you the crown of life."

Furthermore, I propose that the beheadings in Revelation could take place at the Third Temple's altar, ridiculing Jewish sacrificial practices. As Revelation 20:4 foretells:

4 And I saw thrones, and they sat upon them, and judgment was given unto them: and I saw the souls of them that were beheaded for the witness of Jesus, and for the word of God, and which had not worshipped the beast, neither his image, neither had received his mark upon their foreheads, or in their hands; and they lived and reigned with Christ a thousand years.
"

Notice that in the Daniel verses I cited, the references to "and some of those of understanding" and "none of the wicked shall understand, but the wise shall understand" align with the riddle in Revelation 13:18: "*Here is wisdom. Let him who has understanding calculate the number of the beast, for it is the number of a man: His number is 666.*"

Those who possess understanding and wisdom refuse to take the mark of the beast and pay with their lives. They recognize the False Messiah's identity from the beginning and know he is not their savior.

The Bible describes the martyrs in Revelation 12:11: "*And they overcame him by the blood of the Lamb and by the word of their testimony, and they did not love their lives to the death.*"

Revelation 6:9-12 also mentions the martyrs,

each given a white robe. They were slain "*for the word of God and the testimony which they held.*" The martyrs cry out for vengeance against those on earth who took their lives, and God responds, "*that they should rest a little while longer, until both the number of their fellow servants and their brethren, who would be killed as they were, was completed.*"

Abraham's Discussion With God Over Sodom and Gomorrah

God allows the martyrdom of righteous Jews during the Tribulation because of His promise to Abraham. When God was going to destroy Sodom and Gomorrah, Abraham prayed for the city. God let it be known that He would not destroy the city if any righteous people remained. Neither will He destroy the earth if one righteous person remains.

The False Messiah-Antichrist-Accomplishes His Aims

Daniel 7:25 states:
"He shall speak pompous words against the Most High, Shall persecute the saints of the Most High, And shall intend to change times and law. Then the saints shall be given into his hand For a time and times and half a time."

Daniel 7:21 adds: "I was watching; and the same horn was making war against the saints and prevailing against them." The next verse is noteworthy: "until the Ancient of Days came and a judgement was made in favor of the saints of the Most High, and the time came for the saints to possess the kingdom" (this occurs with the destruction of the earth and the return of Christ).

The 1260 Days of Daniel and Revelation

Many verses on the death of saints reference a time frame of "a time, times, and half a time." Revelation 13:
14 states regarding Israel in the wilderness:

"But the woman was given two wings of a great eagle, that she might fly into the wilderness to her place, where she is nourished for a time, times, and half a time, from the presence of the serpent."

This time frame marks the martyrs' killings, completed at the 1260th day, the three-and-a-half-year point, in the second half of the final seven years of Jeremiah's 490 years for Israel.

Biblical Reasons for Martyrdom

Two Biblical reasons explain why Christians being killed during the Tribulation falls in line with Biblical teachings:

1. For the seventh trumpet and the final woe to occur, believers will need to be gone, why? Because if one righteous person remained on the earth, God would not destroy it.
2. Daniel 12:7 states:

"Then I heard the man clothed in linen, who was above the waters of the river, when he held up his right hand and his left hand to heaven, and swore by Him who lives forever, that it shall be for a time, times, and half a time; and when the power of the holy people has been completely shattered, all these things shall be finished."

God's policy, reflected in Abraham's discussion with God (Genesis 18:16-33), is to spare the earth if righteous individuals remain.

The 1290 Days

The significance of persecution and martyrdom is that when the power of the holy people is crushed, the final judgments that culminate in the destruction of the earth can begin. Daniel 12 tells us that there are 1290 days from the abomination of desolation until the end. In this remaining 30 days, God unleashes the worst of the Revelation plagues.

Revelation 12 shows Israel protected in the wilderness for 1260 days. In my book, "The 144 Thousand of Revelation: Explained & Identified-Israel's Haredim," I provide details of how these young men will be able to perform miracles as Moses did in the Wilderness. God will not allow the righteous Jews to suffer any of the Revelation plagues. He will provide for them, but they will be defeated by the False Messiah. This is their plight during the Tribulation. They will face hardship under the persecution of the False Messiah, also known as the Antichrist.

Most likely, they will again be fed manna in the wilderness, under the leadership of the Haredim.

The 1260-Day Ministry of the Two Witnesses

In the 1260-day time frame, the two witnesses of Revelation, believed to be Moses and Elisha or Enoch, warn the world. Revelation predicts that the two witnesses prophesy for 1260 days, after which the third woe and the seventh trumpet will come. The two witnesses' dead bodies lie for three and a half days, and they resurrect before everyone. This coincides with the three-and-a-half-year ministry of Jesus and the timing of His resurrection.

The Antichrist's Reign

The Antichrist, as a false Christ, also has a three-and-a-half-year reign from the day he establishes his deity in the Temple. We see God tell those murdered in Revelation 6:11, "that they should rest a little while longer, until both the number of their fellow servants and their brethren, who would be killed as they were, was completed." This completion takes place on the 1260th day, and at the completion, the two witnesses resurrect back to heaven. When the Antichrist successfully murders the remaining believers, there will no longer be any righteous individuals walking the earth. If any are left, the seventh seal would not launch, or the final woe.

The Final 30 Days Before Armageddon

In the additional 30 days, the angels **unleash**

the seven bowl judgments from the seven trumpets. There is the possibility that the first bowl will overlap and be unleashed while the remaining believers are being murdered. The first bowl falls on those who have taken the mark of the beast, causing pains and loathsome sores.

The Seven Bowl Judgments (Revelation 16:1-21)

1. **Sores on those with the Mark of the** beast
2. The Sea becomes actual blood, and all living creatures die
3. All rivers and springs become actual blood - These plagues are retribution for the martyrs; The Bible explains, "For they have shed the blood of saints and prophets, And you have given them blood to drink. For it is their just due."
4. The sun scorches men with great heat and fire
5. Darkness on the throne of the beast
6. Spirits drawing and gathering armies for the battle of Armageddon
7. A Great earthquake divides cities around the globe, mountains disappear from resulting landslides, and islands fall

into the sea. Meanwhile, the earth gets
pounded with 100-pound hailstones
Support for the 30-Day Time Frame

William F. Dankenbring commented in an
article that God's period of "judgment" will last
"one hour." He further stated, "These ten kings
give their power to the Beast for precisely
'ONE HOUR.'" He asked, "How long is 'one
hour,' speaking prophetically?"

Dankenbring concluded, "Since a 'day'
equals a 'year' in being fulfilled (Num. 14:34;
Ezek. 4:4-6), and since there are 12 months in
a year, this means that 'ONE HOUR' equals
ONE MONTH in being fulfilled! One month
equals 30 days!" Within this time frame, we also
see the destruction of Babylon in Revelation
17.

The Horrors of the Final 30 Days

It's difficult to imagine the horrors of this
final 30-day period. It begins with suffering
from loathsome and painful sores on all those
marked with the mark of the beast. As the last
righteous Jew is murdered, all oceans, seas,
rivers, lakes, streams, and dams will turn to
actual blood, and the life within those bodies

of water will die and pile up on beaches. This is God's retaliation for the killing of His saints for not taking the mark of the beast.

Ecological Disaster

Once the waters turn to blood, and all sea life dies, so will other animal life, causing famine and thirst, alongside the sores. The entire ecosystem will be disrupted, bringing numerous horrors.

Extreme Heat

The sun will become extremely hot, causing fires and burning men, possibly resulting from the sun's nuclear fusion. With no water to quench their thirst, the great heat will cause massive power outages. Men and women will be thirsty, hot, and dealing with their sores.

Rioting and Panic

With the remaining persons on earth, there will be rioting and fighting as people fight and loot for something to drink. Mass panic will ensue.

Drawn Swords

In conclusion, Scripture states regarding the False Messiah's Covenant of Death, "his words were smoother than butter, but they were drawn swords." The rebuilding of the Temple served as a means for the False Messiah to claim it as his own and blaspheme God. The right of return and bringing Jews back to their land enabled him to easily eliminate them as a group. The military agreement within the treaty allowed him to lay siege without resistance, as his military merged with Israel's. The guarantee and association agreement paved the way for the False Messiah to establish Jerusalem as his capital.

Israel has long been the coveted prize in global affairs, and he seized it through this treaty.

It is from his newfound headquarters in Jerusalem that the ultimate battle, Armageddon, unfolds. God permitted the False Messiah's reign as part of the earth's judgments. With the righteous removed from the earth by him, God can destroy the world as we know it today. This also sets the stage for the return of the true Messiah, Jesus Christ, and the millennial kingdom.

ABOUT THE AUTHOR

Erika Grey, author, Bible scholar, commentator, journalist has been a born-again Christian for over 40 years She has written numerous books on Bible Prophecy and made contributions in helping to decode the more difficult forecasts. She has spoken on numerous radio stations including Coast to Coast.

This book is one of a series of short books by Erika Grey intended to be quick reads with important information. Be sure to check out Erika's other titles at www.erikagrey.com.